Easter

Friedrich Benesch

Easter

Floris Books

Translated by Robin and Sibylle Alexander

Originally published in German under the title
Ostern: Passion — Tod — Auferstehung
by Verlag Urachhaus in 1978

© 1978 Verlag Urachhaus, Stuttgart
This translation © Floris Books, Edinburgh, 1981
All rights reserved. No part of this publication may
be reproduced without the prior permission of
Floris Books, 21 Napier Road, Edinburgh.

British Library Cataloguing in Publication Data

Benesch, Friedrich
Easter.
1. Jesus Christ – Passion
2. Jesus Christ – Resurrection
3. Jesus Christ – Crucifixion
I. Title   II. Ostern. *English*
232.9′6   BT400

ISBN 0-903540-44-4

Printed in Great Britain
by Morrison & Gibb Ltd, Edinburgh

Contents

Foreword	6
The Passion of Jesus Christ — Redemptive Power for Man	7
The Sun-Ego of the Son	14
The Wrestling Ego of Man	28
The Cross on Golgotha	42
The Mystery of the Body of Jesus	50
Christ's Resurrection	69

Foreword

We must *feel* Christmas; feel that Christ is there and lives with us on earth. Whitsun must be *willed*. Each has to dedicate his own individuality freely to the spirit.

One has to learn to *think* Easter, because Easter is a happening, a deed, that has suspended the laws of nature about which we think with relative ease. The resurrection of the body is a process that established a new world within the world of natural laws, that planted the strength of the spiritual realm in the sensory realm in order to spiritualize it. It is difficult to think along these lines, but a start must be made. Aid is given to us by Rudolf Steiner in his anthroposophy. With his help, we can learn to think resurrection as we can think of natural phenomena. These essays are devoted to this task. Each one stands under a particular aspect, some are repetitious but it would not be wise to take them out of their context. May they be presented as a beginning towards learning to think in the light of spiritual science, using the many indications which Rudolf Steiner gave us to see the events of the Gospels anew. Perhaps it may stimulate heart and soul to raise the Easter thought into an Easter experience.

The Passion of Jesus Christ Redemptive Power for Man

Centuries ago there lived the exalted teacher of suffering. Old age is suffering; sickness, separation, dying are suffering; bereavement is suffering; enforced parting is suffering. The sayings of the great Buddha, the Gautama Buddha were sending out their light. He saw the cause of suffering in the thirst for existence, because when that ceases, suffering ceases. What does this imply? Is this the way out? It would mean turning away from the earth.

Let us look more closely. What is suffering in the form of physical pain? That unique throbbing, or stabbing, or burning, or consuming physical pain. Into what kind of a world are we immersed here? Or let us look at mental suffering — grief, worry, sorrow, deprivation — and finally spiritual pain. The existence of this is questioned. But it does exist. Faust suffered purely spiritual pain in his confrontation with the enigma of the world, the impossibility of solving the riddle of mankind. Or think of the purely spiritual experience of the meaninglessness of existence that can torture a man or woman today.

What do we enter into when we are immersed in physical pain, mental suffering and pain, and spiritual pain?

Not only human beings share in the world of pain. Modern spiritual science has established that every kind of crystallization or hardening is accompanied by pain and that in the plant world the plucking of green leaves is pleasure but the pulling up of roots gives pain. And who knows how the innocent animal suffers? Is the world of suffering a reality or only the subjective experience of certain beings? Or is suffering a world substance? In the supersensory world is found the age-old struggle of adversaries against the good gods. Are they 'happy' thereby? We may ask, what do the good spiritual beings experience? Do the angels share in suffering according to their relationship to the human beings whom they guide? Would an angel experience pain through the conduct of men? We may dare to say that there is no realm and no being that does not share in the world and the substance of pain.

We ask what happens within the being who suffers? We see the worm double up and contract when stepped upon. In this quality of pain which permeates the whole universe there is concealed an immense power of contraction and concentration. In mental suffering there is the same concentration; nothing deepens the soul as much as suffering. In suffering a person has to grow inwardly and this leads to the formation of a fruit which has the quality of depth. Experiences which are wrought with pain have an 'enduring' quality. Through concentration our experience is deepened and remains within us, not just as a fleeting mood but as consciousness. It stays with us as a guarantee of the highest form of consciousness which, through the ages, has been called *wisdom*. Not those experiences which are spread out or exhibited but those which turn us inward and deepen our soul are really our very own possession. The harvest of suffering and pain is — concentration — deepening

— inwardness — individualized experience — wisdom.

If we now look at the Passion of Jesus Christ, we find a renewed understanding of his suffering. From the Christian tradition of Holy Week images emerge for our inner eye: Jesus taken prisoner and abused during interrogation, the scourging, the crowning with thorns, the carrying of the cross, the crucifixion, his burning thirst, the sponge with vinegar, his last breath and finally death itself — all these outward events have the most profound hidden meaning. Behind the outer appearance, unhindered by sentimentality one can observe how this Passion held sway throughout the three and a quarter years that Christ walked on earth. It is difficult for us to feel our way into the experience this being must have had, every time he met a man or a woman! Each meeting was a kind of suffering on behalf of others, not just in extreme cases when he was hated and slandered or in the less extreme instances when he was misunderstood or not recognized. Every time he was confronted with a human being he suffered because of what mankind had become.

Rudolf Steiner has revealed in the *Fifth Gospel** how Jesus, before he became the Christ, walked the earth as an innocent human being, suffering the Fall of mankind. This is a special form of suffering, a compassion or suffering-on-behalf-of. Ordinary people may suffer deeply but only this being had the ability to fathom the depths, the truth and the reality

---

* Rudolf Steiner, *The Fifth Gospel*, Rudolf Steiner Press, London 1968.

of pain in others and so bring to light what had been unconscious. Thus he who suffers our suffering more deeply than we do ourselves walks among us.

As soon as we comprehend this we have to admit that we are unable to have such a vicarious experience because every form of our suffering is caused by ourselves. But in Jesus the personal participation in suffering is zero, this suffering-on-behalf-of is complete. With deep humility we perceive this mystery, which St Paul describes in the Letter to the Philippians (2:5-8).

> Try to find the same inner attitude as Christ Jesus, who from the very beginning subsisted in a divine form but did not claim this divinity for himself, did not claim to be a divine being but, emptying himself, took on the form of a servant and became a human being. And being found in human form, he humbled himself and became subject to the law of death, even the death on the cross.

In order to grasp the immensity of this event we need a concept for its dimensions and its intensity. We find its significance when we look away from the earth out into the universe and perceive Christ as a divine cosmic being.

We see the sun that journeys through the cosmos like a breathing, pulsating, radiant being. A telescope shows a kind of 'granulation' on the sun's surface. It is a picture of flames, whose base is about the size of Spain and Portugal together and whose height is the distance from Panama to Alaska. Imagine a candle flame of such dimensions! These colossal flames burn continuously, they leap up, remain for some minutes.

As one dies down the next appears. Thousands upon thousands of such flames cover the whole surface of the sun.

The diameter of the sun is one hundred and nine times that of the earth. This huge structure may be regarded as the fire and light body of a being whose dimensions inwardly are identical with the external dimensions of the sun. This is the Christ-being and his cosmic body.

Before the Christ made the sun his body it had a totally different form, namely that of the whole starry universe. There is not a single star which has not been a jewel in the cloak of the Christ.

What Paul says about it is so great, so powerful, so divinely magnificent. An interpretation could read:

From the beginning he was a being of divine form and power, but he did not claim this divine form for himself, but sacrificed it step by step. Sacrificed it inasmuch as he contracted into the sun — that is still gigantic — then he left the sun behind like an outer garment — contracting ever more until he could live in the sphere of the earth. Finally at the Baptism this being entered a human body, replacing the human ego.

What does this self-renunciation, this *kenōsis* as Paul calls it, entail? Rudolf Steiner's *Fifth Gospel* states clearly that the pain which the Christ had to bear on his way from heaven to earth was inconceivably great. After such suffering he becomes a being more profound than any other, and through his sacrifice, renunciation and contraction is able to approach every pain with the attitude, 'I know this at a deeper level, this is not new to me, I have gone through it before.'

After the Baptism in the Jordan, we see the Christ in immeasurable pain caused by contraction — the Passion of Christ — and looking upon the human soul of Jesus, with its capacity for pure empathy for the spiritual suffering of all mankind — the Passion of Jesus.

Christ's Passion is not only the events of Holy Week but the complete absorption of the true essence of suffering, of contraction, deepening, intensification which leads to the essence of selflessness.

All pain has suddenly a new inner substance — a new voluntary character is expressed. The world's suffering as understood by Buddha follows from necessity and is always a reaction to a polar opposite, the chain of karmic law, originating in the craving for existence. Through the deed of Christ something streams into the world of suffering. The Christ not only suffered in entire freedom, selflessness and purely for the sake of others, but he embraced pain completely so that it entered his being and became part of his substance. In this way an impulse is carried over to mankind. Through inner contemplation of Christ a faculty grows within man which overcomes the instinct to avoid suffering. An inner readiness comes about to say 'Yes' to suffering, seeing it as a necessity in the destiny of man not to flee but to face it freely out of an inner connection with the Christ and to identify suffering with one's own being.

There is a fundamental difference between our *having* to suffer and suffering willed by us. Only through our willingness does it become fruitful. A substance is then created in the universe holding all the human experiences of pain that deepen the soul. Christ's voluntary passion leads mankind to embrace pain freely, beyond what is demanded by necessity.

Christ attached a new value to suffering for the whole cosmos, including man. The message of the great Buddha, that the cause of suffering is craving for existence which has to be overcome so that suffering may cease, no longer holds. But recognizing suffering as a necessity and embracing it willingly leads to a spiritual metamorphosis of pain. In this way suffering does not come to an end because the craving for existence has died down, but it becomes the substance of an intensified, renewed individual existence.

Since the mystery of Golgotha three things have become possible within man. First, we come close to Christ through our suffering, whether we suffer through the world or ourselves. Secondly, by nearing Christ, we may take up his Passion freely and without self-pity. Thirdly, we create within our suffering an individual future. Nothing belongs to ourselves as fully as our experience of destiny. Finally we learn that whatever we suffer, Christ suffers with us.

Christ makes no appeal to the human egotism or to the fear which would avoid pain. He speaks to our courage and reveals its meaning. The Passion of Christ is not redemption *from* suffering but redemption *to* suffering, the womb for the birth of the new man. Novalis expresses this with the words: 'Out of pain the new world will be born.'

The Sun-Ego of the Son

> Christ is arisen!
> Joy to the mortal,
> Whom the corrupting,
> Creeping, hereditary
> Imperfections enveloped.
> Goethe, *Faust*

The Easter message of Christ's resurrection is a call to joy. It is also a call to understand the mystery of Golgotha and the resurrection of Jesus Christ as a physical event which is a spiritual deed accomplished by a spiritual being, the Son.

There are important moments in history when mankind perceives reality. On March 11, 1832 a student visited his master. He had an English Bible in his hand and protested that the edition omitted several books which he had loved since childhood, maintaining they were not genuine, for example the Book of Tobit. A conversation ensued, which he subsequently wrote down. The master's answer as to what is or is not genuine in the Bible, particularly the New Testament, was as follows:

> Regarding the Bible, the question of true or false is rather curious. What is truth but excellence, that which is in harmony and reason and serves our highest development to this day! What is false but the absurd, shallow and stupid that brings no fruit.... I hold all four Gospels to be

true because there is a radiance of nobility in them which streams from Christ and is of such divine quality as has ever appeared on earth. If I am asked does it lie in my nature to revere him, I say, yes indeed. I bow down before him as a divine revelation of the highest principal of morality. If I am asked whether it is in my nature to revere the sun, I say again, yes, because the sun is also a revelation of the highest, the most powerful one granted to us children of the earth. I worship the light in it and the creative power of God through which we live and have our being, and all plants and animals with us.*

Why is this such a special moment? Because in this conversation, when the Son of God is mentioned, Goethe talks about the *sun*. Separate at first, the two suddenly stand side by side, equally revered. Such ideas are stimulating for us. It is helpful to observe the sun when we wish to look at the ego, the 'I' of Christ. Jesus used parables from nature to reveal spiritual realities to people. The kingdom of God is like a man who sowed good seed on his field: the seed, falling on the earth and growing in different ways, helps us to understand a process within the soul of man. Similarly we may look at the sun as a parable for the 'I' of Christ, because the resurrection is a physical fact which originated within his divine 'I'.

Around the sun-being burns a field of giant flames. Its corona becomes visible for us when the sun is darkened by the moon: heat glowing from a sea of fire. Powerful forces send electro-magnetic waves

* Johann Peter Eckermann (1792–1854), *Conversations with Goethe*.

through space, so intensive, violent and dangerous that we have to be protected from burning by the magnetic field of the earth. Only the ozone sphere within the atmosphere saves us from this radiation. If the earth did not possess a protective layer there would be no life on it.

We see the sun as a being of fire, a being of power and a being of light. We should not understand this light simply as electro-magnetic vibrations; it is also a wonderful ethereal light, giving to the earth with its air, cloudscapes and continents when seen from outer space a most delicate blue colour. This light wafts around the earth, keeping pace with the earth's movement, and spans a bow of colours across the sky.

Our senses perceive the sun as a threefold outer being: of fire, of power, of blessedly glowing coloured light. The sun is not only out there where we see it, it is also with us. In earlier times mankind was able to find beyond the physical sun another totally different one, discernible even through the material earth. Rudolf Steiner characterizes the difference between the physical and the spiritual sun with the verses:

> Asleep is the soul of Earth
> In Summer's heat,
> While the Sun's outward Glory
> Rays through the realms of Space.
>
> Awake is the Soul of Earth
> In Winter's cold,
> While the Sun's inmost Being
> Lightens in Spirit.*

---

* Rudolf Steiner, *Verses and Meditations*, p. 65, Rudolf Steiner Press, London 1972.

The classical Greeks had a completely different relationship to the sun from that of modern science. In the atmospheric light between Greece and Asia Minor, from Crete to the Bosporus and even to the Ionian Islands, in the rose-coloured gleaming light, the Greeks experienced a threefold sun-being in which an archangel breathed and worked, carrying phosphorescent light in his soul. They saw an 'imagination', a spiritual being called Zeus who ruled the ether, and in the beams of the rose-coloured light, ruled Apollo, the son of Zeus. The chariot of the sun riding across the sky was experienced as Helios, son of the Titans. Three generations of gods participated to make the sun externally visible. This is the world of spiritual beings, in Christian terminology, of angels, archangels and archai.

Earlier, in the cultural period of Egypt, the being behind the sun-chariot was called Ra, and later addressed as Aton. The quality of this sun-god is a radiance flowing from the cosmos to earth, but in contrast to Helios, is perceived from a spiritual aspect. Aton appears as a being of the hierarchy of the Dynameis, who are spirits of movement. Their offspring is Osiris who changes from being a sun-god of day to being a sun-god of night. It is his son, Horus, who bears the individualized forces of the sun that come to birth in the initiate. Here again, we have generations of hierarchical beings.

The people of the Old Testament saw the Elohim, the Exousiai. They are sun-beings and Spirits of Form standing at the beginning of creation, who send forth one of their number, Yahweh the ruler of the moon. They are revealed through the Archangel Michael.

In a civilization preceding all these, the Persians, the people of the sun, had as their great initiate Zarathustra. Among the spirits of the sun he saw the Kyriotetes, spirits of wisdom, and in their midst the highest, the sun-spirit Ahura Mazdao who revealed himself to men through an archangel — Mithras.

Our senses reach out to the threefold outer sun: the fiery being of flames; the radiant being of power; and the light being. Behind is the supersensory threefold sun: the ranks of archangels of the sun; the creative sun-gods, of the Elohim or Exousiai, Dynameis, Kyriotetes; and the highest sun-being, Ahura Mazdao.

The sensitive perception of earlier epochs evoked the question: What is the outer sun, as an expression of active divine beings? Is it something in itself, or is it there only because these beings are working together? How does the wonderful appearance come about? Atomic science conceives an 'atomic oven', in which hydrogen is continuously changed to helium and helium to an even denser gas, setting free enormous energies. One can imagine that such processes take place on the surface of the sun. But wherein lies the true process that created the sun in the cosmos?

Spiritual science likens the outer sun to an enormous cosmic magnifying glass, a focal point in which all the energy, heat and light of the cosmos is concentrated and distributed again. This is an energy picture of the sun. But the sun comes into being only through the activities of the spiritual beings who dwell where we perceive fixed stars. From the ground of all creation these send forth thoughts, feelings and will power directed to the sun. This is a totally different picture from that of the astronomers.

Impulses of energy ray out from these spiritual beings, from the divine source within the cosmos, to the sun and there penetrate each other, interweave and create archetypes, blueprints for all forms of life. From the sun as a focal point these forces then stream out to the planets, Neptune, Uranus, Jupiter and Saturn, Mars, Venus and Mercury, which receive them, and reflect them again, spiritually transformed according to the planet's motion around the sun. Then with all that has been united with the essence of the planets these forces concentrate again in the sun and then radiate through the solar system as far as the earth which among the planets has a special place, as life only manifests itself here. From the earth the forces are reflected to the sun a third time and thence right out to all the planets and the stars.

The cosmic being of the sun shows a threefold breathing in and out of energy, images and impulses: from the circumference of the stars into the sun and out to the planets; from the planets into the sun and out to the earth; and from the earth into the sun and out to all the planets and stars again.

In this process the earth is unique, for it catches the rays, the images and impulses and without returning them as do the other planets, particularly the moon, takes them deeply into itself and brings forth stones, plants, animals and people — a living mirror, it reflects the sun's life as earthly life.

> See thou, mine eye,
> The Sun's pure rays
> In crystal forms of Earth.

> See thou, my heart,
> The Sun's Spirit-power
> In Water's surging wave.
>
> See thou, my soul,
> The Sun's cosmic will
> In quivering gleam of Air.
>
> See thou, my Spirit,
> The Sun's indwelling God
> In Fire's abounding love.*

Earth, water, air, fire — the earth elements — are stimulated by the sun, so that they reflect the life of the sun in myriad forms. Why does our heart rejoice when we walk into nature in May? The sky may be overcast, but still the sun shines from below and when the clouds have passed how brilliant is nature! The true being of the sun is the place in the universe where all the energies of the world are gathered, taken in, rayed out, reabsorbed and mirrored back, returning to where they came from. Most intensive and concentrated, at the same time most selfless. Goethe compared the central figure of the Gospels with the sun, but he did not see the sun just as a likeness. For him both were revelations.

> Sun, thou radiance-bearer,
> the power over matter of thy light
> conjures life out of the earth's
> immeasurably rich depths.

---

* Rudolf Steiner, *Verses and Meditations*, p. 141

> Heart, thou soul-bearer,
> the spirit power of thy light
> conjures life out of man's
> immeasurable inner depths.
>
> When I look at the sun
> its light speaks radiantly
> of the spirit who walks
> through beings of the world with mercy.
>
> When I feel in my heart,
> the spirit speaks its own true word
> of man whom he loves
> through all time and eternally.
>
> Looking up I can see
> in the sun's round brightness
> the mighty heart of the world.
> Looking inward I can feel
> in the heart's warm beat
> man's sun ensouled.*

In this verse, the inner identity between heart and sun, man and cosmos is expressed.

If we now try with due reverence to penetrate the Christ being, the cosmic ego or 'I' through the sun metaphor, what do we find?

Is it not the case that an 'I' is real when there is a continuous activity going out from it into the world, when it is acting and creating? Conversely, it is only an 'I' in the moment when enriching experiences

---

* Rudolf Steiner, *Wahrspruchworte*, Rudolf Steiner Verlag, Dornach 1978.

come into it from the world, enlarging and amplifying it. In the relationship between 'I' and world, world and 'I', we see the first two basic processes of the ego.

The 'I' can also be orientated towards the spirit and impart something to it; conversely inspiration from the spirit can work into the 'I'.

But the 'I' to be genuine must meet and be met by brothers on an equal footing, so that the relationship of 'I' and 'I' can arise.

Finally we find the interaction from the world *through* the 'I' to the spirit; and from the spirit, *through* the 'I', to the world.

Summing up, there are seven relationships: from the 'I' to the world, from the world to the 'I', from the 'I' to the spirit, from the spirit to the 'I', from 'I' to 'I', from the world through the 'I' to the spirit and from the spirit through the 'I' to the world. In these seven basic transactions the life of the 'I' is realized.

These processes resemble those on the sun. It is characteristic of the sun that it absorbs what streams into it from its surroundings, transforms it and sends it out to the planets which ray it back into the sun, whence it is radiated to the earth and then back to the sun and finally returned to the fixed stars from where it originally came.

Mankind is still only on the way to understanding how to develop the 'I' in this complete sevenfold manner. Yet such an 'I' was once a man on earth. Since then it has lived with us on earth as the 'I' of the resurrected one, the perfect divine-human sevenfold ego of Christ.

In St John's Gospel we find the revelation of this sevenfold 'I' in the seven 'I am' sayings.

'I am the bread of life.' One could also say, my 'I', the true 'I' is in the first ray of Christ's being, the bread of life. The 'I' gives nourishment to the world.

The second saying 'I am the light of the world' does not refer to ordinary light, which is sunlight become external. The light that radiates from the 'I' of Christ is the consciousness of his union with the Father. From the Father through the 'I' into the world streams the light that I am.

The Christ being has not left us in the slightest doubt as to how 'I' and 'I' are related to one another. He came into the earthly world as a human being and he lived among men as a human being. He said to his disciples 'No longer do I call you servants, for the servant does not know what his master is doing; but I have called you friends . . . ' The sun 'I' of the Son becomes brotherly when it comes in contact with the egos of other men, and pervades them. This great 'I' is the door from 'I' to 'I'. Whoever does not come to the 'I' through the 'I' is a thief.

Closely linked with this is the saying of the Good Shepherd. Human egos are in the world. Inasmuch as the Christ 'I' accompanies them, it guards them and helps them to come out of the world, each to his I. Just as the Christ ego in the bread gives life to the world, it radiates as the Good Shepherd from the world into the ego — and from the egos of human beings to his 'I'.

The following 'I am' sayings are related to the resurrection. One of them is spoken at the raising of Lazarus. 'I am the resurrection and the life.' As soon as the 'I' wakens to the spirit there follows the movement towards the spirit; the 'I' awakes and becomes radiant, the 'I' itself becomes spirit and is united to the spiritual — the human 'I' in Christ's ego. The resurrection in the 'I'; the 'I' itself is resurrection.

Then in the farewell discourse comes, 'I am the way, the truth and the life.' The way is from without inwards, the spiritual working upon the 'I'; the truth shines forth in the 'I' as spiritual reality; and finally the spirit will live in the 'I'. In the last saying we considered the 'I' that would live in the spirit, now we are concerned with the spirit that will live in the 'I'.

The last saying speaks of the Father as the vinedresser and the Son as the true vine, the human egos are the branches. If they remain attached to the vine they produce spiritual fruits. The world is a vineyard and what enters from it into the 'I' in the right way is so transformed that it can be given back as fruit, indeed the whole world can be returned to the Father from whom it issued. From the world, through the I, to the spirit, to the Father.

The 'I' of the Son travels in majestic inner movement over the earth as the sun. Who is the Son himself, if the 'I' of the Son is such that life pulsates from him to the world and from the world to him, that life breathes from him to the spirit and back to him, and that life comes from brother to brother, from 'I' to 'I', and finally that life flows from the spirit through the ego to the world and from the world through the ego to the spirit? Christ has not given a direct answer, but he has summed up the being of the divine sun nature in the dynamic process of the sevenfold movement of the ego.

'As the Father has loved me, so have I loved you;

abide in my love. If you keep my commandments, you will abide in my love, just as I have kept my Father's commandments and abide in his love' (John 15:9f). The Father in me, I in the Father, I in you and you in me. This 'in me', 'in him', and 'in you', is not absolute static being but bears within it the attributes of Christ's names. For the names of Christ are themselves the revelation of his 'I': the Son; the Word; the Lord; the Anointed — the Christ; the Saviour; the Sacrificial Lamb. When we let these names speak to us he reveals himself as the Son born in eternity of the Father; the world creator, the Logos, the Word; the stimulator of the 'I', the lord of the 'I'; the penetrator of the human 'I'; the Saviour, the healer of the world; the one who is continuously sacrificed.

The more spiritually we understand the sun, the better able are we to understand the sayings about the 'I' in the Gospels, the more closely sun and Gospel are drawn together. Goethe sensed closeness in his veneration but he still placed them side by side. The sun is the corresponding body of the Son, the Son is the true spirit of the sun.

What is the origin of their intimate connection? It must lie in the nature of the collector and distributor of rays.

It is appropriate at this point to introduce something belonging to the higher levels of spiritual science. In his lectures *Man in the Light of Occultism, Thesophy and Philosophy**, Rudolf Steiner describes how the present cosmos arose out of earlier more spiritual

---

* Rudolf Steiner Press, London 1964.

conditions in which the physical-sensory and the spiritual-supersensory were more closely interrelated, and the form of that older creation conditioned the sun of the planetary system. The clairvoyant perceives two related beings. We are grateful to Rudolf Steiner for showing us the origin of the Christ 'I' in the sun. He describes conditions on the Old Sun where two spiritual brothers who closely resemble one another stand opposite — Lucifer and Christ.

Lucifer, on the one side, the ruler of Venus, is an extraordinarily luminous figure (we mean spiritual light) giving the impression that all radiance that can ever reach us through any perception of light is somewhat trivial compared with the majesty of Lucifer at the time of the Old Sun. But when we investigate Lucifer's intentions we see a spirit endowed with pride, such infinite pride that can lead us into temptation. Things which would normally not tempt us become tempting when raised to majestic dimensions. Lucifer's temptation lies in the pride of his great brilliance. He possesses 'unrevealed' light that does not shine outwardly but has great power in itself.

On the other side stands the Christ, the ruler of the sun planet, an image of complete devotion to the world, dedicated to all that surrounds him in the universe.

This wide universe was not then as it is today. If one were on the sun today one would see the twelve constellations of the zodiac. But they were not then present in this external form. Indeed there were twelve beings who spoke their words out of the depths of darkness. What were these words? These were words (and 'word' is really an inadequate expression) that spoke of ancient times. These were twelve world initiators. Today, in their place stand the twelve constellations of the Zodiac which speak to the soul the unspoken cosmic Word which was formed by twelve voices. While Lucifer had the urge to illuminate everything in order *thereby* to know it, Christ gave himself up to the hidden primeval word and took it completely into himself. The mystery of the universe was united with Christ's soul. Christ's receiving the primeval Word contrasts with proud Lucifer's rejecting the Word and wishing to establish everything with his own light.

This is a spiritual image of the sun-ego of the Son of God. Everything is concentrated here, everything radiates out from here. Because Christ is devoted to the Word of the spiritual beings he becomes the bearer of the Logos, becomes the Word himself.

If we want to experience the power of Christ not only as Lord of the sun but also as Son of the Father God, then we may discern the sevenfold ego unified and centring its divine activity. It is the most profound power of the divine that would unite with the most profound power of man. It is love in which the true sun being of the Son moves.

The Wrestling Ego of Man

Having contemplated some of the mysteries of the Christ and the sun, we shall now turn to the human side. First, we look at the kingdoms of nature. Minerals are characterized by the physical body of stones, plants by the life that is added, in animals this living body is permeated with soul. Then we come to the human being who has an 'I'. The difficulty begins here, for to be an 'I' and to have an 'I', to be existentially conscious of nature and the creation, and not only to have the 'I' but to manipulate it — this is a stratified process.

Work on the 'I' is strenuous. People cannot come to terms with the 'I' at all because they ask: What is this 'I', in me or on me or with me? We cannot experience this 'I' except in our consciousness. This raises the next question, is it consciousness that is the 'I' or is this consciousness in which we live when awake only a vessel in which all our experiences take place, from outer experience through thoughts, ideas, memories, emotions, desires and passions, right through to actions of will? We carry the whole content of our life and experience in this consciousness. Is this the 'I'? Or must a self-consciousness arise within it for an experience or an idea to be possible? How does consciousness come about in the first place? How do we experience it lighting up in the morning, becoming the unified space both within and without where everything unfolds and where in the evening everything is extinguished in sleep? Where, within consciousness, does our self awareness lie? Here we come to something mysterious. The fact that we are aware of ourselves does not depend on direct perception of the ego in daily life. I say, 'I am thinking,' and it is the thinking I am conscious of, not myself. The 'I' remains in the background. It seems that the continuity of all our experience is held together by the memories we have. But are these connected experiences concerned with the 'I' or with the awareness of the 'I', that is, with self-perception?

The answer to this mystery is exciting. Through sleep a hiatus takes place in the continuous stream of consciousness, an intrusion of unconsciousness. It is just here, where sleep interrupts the chain of experience that the 'I' with all the day's experiences is hidden. The real identification of myself with myself arises only through my unconsciously becoming aware of these mighty gaps; sleep's dark, bottomless hole, unconsciousness within the illuminated fullness of my experience.

The consciousness of 'I' arises within consciousness because we have a minus-awareness behind which our 'I' is concealed and out of which we then say, 'I am walking', 'I am thinking', — but it is the walking and thinking I observe, not the 'I'; that remains in the background.

Asking how the 'I' that stands behind our mental images appears when we have an experience, we find that when man experiences, understands and absorbs something new, the 'I' does not appear; as soon, however, as something appears incomprehensible to which he cannot relate then this incomprehensibility is reported to the 'I'. If I understand something so that I am completely absorbed and it fills my whole attention, the 'I' remains in the background forgotten. When, however, I am involved in something I do not understand, the 'I' suddenly intrudes. The 'I' works behind the ideas, the thoughts and perceptions. It is the same with desires. If they are met then they and their satisfaction absorb my consciousness; if they are not met, then, at once the 'I' is noticeable.

Added to this awareness of the 'I', to this self-perception, which is so unclear and undefined, is our self-feeling. Every impulse of will and every thought we think, and also most of our perceptions are linked to emotions. This is known in psychology as 'affective experience' and provides emotional colour to ideals, intentions and thoughts. It has a strong subjective quality because when I think of something I do not necessarily suggest that it is I who think; I simply think it. When I assert my will I do not consider that it is I who am willing, I simply will. But the nature of feeling is subjective. I not only feel, but I feel that I feel. It is not just a question of simple emotion but of a movement in the soul that it refers to itself, so that in every feeling, I am aware of subjectivity and of my self.

While it is only when not comprehending that we notice the 'I' behind our thinking and in discontent, behind our wanting and wishing, there is, in the subjectivity and egocentricity of the emotional life, a middle ground in which the 'I' participates and comes to the surface of experience. We have the 'I' that lives behind mental images, behind and above us, the 'I' that lives behind our will below and behind us, while the 'I' that lives in feeling, is present in our heart.

Self-perception and self-feeling are heightened the moment we affirm something. As soon as we do so, the 'I' appears in the foreground of our soul. This is the point when man really enters into self-consciousness through perception of his 'I'. Self-feeling has still something dormant about it, but in judgment and assertion, as Fichte wrote, the 'I' stands in the foreground. A judgment can only arise through the 'I'. When I say 'yes' or 'no' it is said by me. Self-consciousness can indeed only be based on the ability to make a statement, to make a judgment.

Considering the possible variations of affirmative and negative judgment, we see that firstly there are intellectual judgments. A concept can be illuminated by means of other concepts, for example: freedom is self-determination. This is a judgment of pure thought, concept is linked to concept.

Secondly, we make judgments that link concept to percept, for example: the tree is green. We have the concept tree and the percept tree, the concept green and the percept green. We link concepts with percepts and form a judgment of perception.

The third form goes beyond the judgments of thought and perception. We can say, 'the green tree *is*'. That is a judgment of existence and not only expresses a state of affairs, a context of thought but also affirmation and acknowledgement of reality. I make an existential judgment that ascribes reality to the state of affairs and say such and such *is*, exists. This existential judgment can only be made by one who is able to give himself existence. I cannot say the tree is, the star is, good is, if I do not in the same breath make the judgment, he who says this also exists, and I am he.

The judgment, 'I am', has evolved gradually throughout human history. Two historical figures in particular show man wrestling with self-consciousness. St Augustine, in the search for God, went through profound doubt. He could say, 'One thing is certain: I can doubt everything, but that I doubt is certain and therefore the doubter himself is certain'.

Similarly, Descartes about a thousand years later said, 'I think, therefore I am'. Both arrive at ego-consciousness, in the sense that they attribute existence to their 'I'. When, therefore, the existential judgment is made regarding the tree, the tree is, or the green tree is, then the existential judgment is expressed that relates to one's own ego, not merely my 'I' is, but, 'I am'. This is not a sense perception, neither is it a feeling, nor an item of knowledge, but a judgment, and an affirmation.

The moment a person says, 'I am' and not, 'I am this or that' or, 'I feel', 'I know', 'I think', 'I will', or 'I perceive', and not even, 'my I is', in that moment there is a real confrontation of the 'I' with itself. Only a spiritual, thinking, judging being can make this act of self-determination, self-judgment. As long as people do not learn to say with full reality, in decisive moments of their lives, 'I am', just so long will there be no self-consciousness in the true sense.

We see at once there is a struggle in man to move out of self-perception that is yet dormant and arises through negation, through self-feeling which is less dormant but still imprecise, to self-knowledge in the form of self-affirmation.

The three elements, self-perception, self-feeling, self-knowledge, interact continually in the biography of every man. They develop in seven remarkable stages.

In the third or fourth year the child says 'I' for the first time, not I *am*, but *I*, I want to, I will not, I walk, and so on. All at once, the perception of the self is taken up into language, streaming into words, stimulated from without because people around the child continually say, I and you, not merely using names. The first experience of 'I' arises because the child, in its identification with his body, gains self-perception. We must pay attention to a decisive moment when the impulse to this awareness of the 'I' arises from the body. The ego is mirrored in this bodily consciousness and the child becomes aware of himself and able to feel, to think and finally to judge. The bodily organization of man has a fundamental significance for the 'I', for self-perception, self-feeling and consciousness. One cannot say the 'I' is the body nor is it the soul or consciousness, but in all three it is either reflected or awakened. The first breakthrough of the 'I' experience takes place in the three-year-old child so that a definite 'Yes', and also a definite 'No' can emerge. Both in 'yes' and in 'no' this wonderful 'I' is felt. (There are some mothers who never come to terms with this 'No'.)

This magical beginning does not last. Six years later, when the child is nine, the second phase sets in. The child can now experience the 'I' as ego for the first time. A classical instance of this can be found in Jean Paul who tells how as a boy he was standing by the wood-shed when it struck him like a flash of lightning 'I am an I!' In this experience I am not the others! The small child still believes I am also the others, I am the chair that annoys me, the table that bumps my head. This merging of 'I' with the world finally ends with the ninth year, and brings loneliness. Many children then get the idea, 'I am not my parent's child, I am a foundling'. Isolation comes with the experience of the 'I'.

In the fourteenth year, at puberty, when the soul becomes independent, the ego-experience is so strong that a young person can feel: I am truly an 'I', the 'I' is hidden in my soul, I must protect it from the world. This mood brings with it a wonderful inwardness and at the same time a second onset of loneliness.

Several years later, at the age of about seventeen or nineteen comes a wonderful breakthrough. He feels that he is lord of his thoughts and can think what he will. He can expound his thoughts to others, have discussion with them and make independent judgments. Have we not all seen young students cornering the most erudite professor? At this age the ego can feel its mastery of ideas and thoughts, and wishes it were also master of its passions. Strong tensions arise between the experience of the ego as master and in its natural weakness. This explains why young people behave so boisterously. Rather than condemn them we should look behind their attitudes to discern the cause. One must accept this self-expression for what it is, a triumph of freedom, of the ego's mastery over thought, the first release from the isolation that arose at fourteen.

A little later, at twenty-one, the decisive experience begins. The young person stands up inwardly saying, 'I have become master of my thoughts, now I want to have mastery over myself. I not only want to think freely, to judge for myself, I also want to rule over myself and be ruled by no-one else!' The so-called adult phase of humanity is at first justifiably anti-authoritarian. Students are not anti-authoritarian by chance but because the ego is experienced as wanting to determine itself and to guide its own affairs — whether it can do this is another question, but to desire it is natural. One often hears a twenty-year-old say, 'I know what I don't want, namely all of *you*!' But what he does want is much more difficult to say, because the true 'I' is not yet quite present.

Thus the human being manoeuvres past some difficult corners to reach twenty-six or twenty-eight. As we experience isolation in the fourteenth year, a breakthrough at seventeen, and both a breakthrough and isolation at twenty-one, so in the twenty-sixth to twenty-eighth year it is a fact that the 'I' experiences what it is *not*. Fichte developed his philosophy on the basis of this gap and tried to reach the real ego-experience, a consciousness of the 'I'. Around the twenty-eighth year everything that hitherto has been taken for granted comes to an end. As youth draws to a close the ego loosens from its sheath — at least this is what it feels like — and in this way the crisis of the middle years arrives. An icy cold loneliness may be felt.

Each must follow the star on his own. All previous feelings of loneliness of the ego are 'on the way'. Around thirty-three and thirty-five, self-knowledge, self-feeling and self-perception are brought into equilibrium and the existential question arises: I am an 'I' but where do I go from here? Until now the 'I' functioned by itself; though outside my control, it nevertheless guided my life and carried me even when I had no notion of why or how. This attitude to life comes to an abrupt end. Where do I stand now? The actual struggle of the 'I' in self-knowledge, self-feeling and self-perception leads to a pure experience in which man becomes aware that he is absolutely alone. With regard to what *I* now do no other person can help me, with regard to what *I* want, I cannot be replaced. I alone am responsible. But how do I cope with it?

Out of this *how* the real struggle of man's ego arises. He discovers that the isolation and loneliness is an illusion; there are two other beings deeply interested in this 'I'.

One of them continually approaches, saying: 'You are somebody, you have your value within youself, your existence is in you and you can do everything yourself! Strengthen this self, strengthen your will and then you will be important!'

So one notices — or fails to notice — that self-consciousness is turning to pride, egocentricity, and that arrogance, ambition and intolerance combine in this pride. In anthroposophy this power is known as Luciferic.

The other power is the Ahrimanic, which has the opposite effect. It confronts a person with his weakness, his impotence and inferiority, and it is right every time! The human soul is finally convinced that this power is justified, and deep depression, a profound feeling of inferiority tries to strangle the 'I'. It is necessary to delineate the two extremes precisely; they are not equally manifest in everybody, yet their tug-of-war is present in all of us while we are developing an ego-consciousness out of our personal 'I'.

Great souls bear witness to this fact in Christian history. Pascal asked, 'What would have become of man had Christ not entered human evolution?' And he wrote: Man is exposed to two dangers. One lies in his experience of the divine in his 'I' as belonging to himself, and as endowed with a kind of divine knowledge. If he experiences the divine only in himself, he is led to pride and destroys his best qualities hardening them within himself.

The other danger lies in denying the spirituality and divinity of the 'I', or failing to find it. Then attention is drawn to the weakness and impotence of the ego and to human misery; this is followed by despair.

The human 'I' stands in the centre of the struggle so that it not only wrestles to attain to *itself*, but also to sustain its true value. This leads our consideration away from man to the question of Christ. the Christ-consciousness is absolutely necessary to a full development of human consciousness! Why is this so? Because without a Christ-consciousness the human 'I' becomes no more than at best a self. It never comes into its own for inwardly it is always filled with other powers, other beings, who falsify the yes or no that belong to the being of the 'I' through the powers of self-assertion or self-abnegation. The genuine 'I' is not present in any other stages, in self-perception, or in self-feeling or in self-knowledge. When we develop these three what is present in us as conscious content is only the reflection of the true being of ourselves. And this gives us our freedom. We are free even from our own real being.

Where is the human 'I'? It is not to be found where self-consciousness is. One must distinguish between self and 'I'. The perception, feeling and consciousness or knowledge of self are the lower self, but also the free self. But where is my true 'I'? It stretches from where my ego radiates into reality, developing my self, to where I wrestle with the Adversaries for the content of this self.

We have established that the real ego exists as our ideals above and behind our thoughts, and is behind the impulses of will as our pure free will, still undirected towards anything specific; that is to say it is not yet determined. If Christ-consciousness illumines a person and he desires to bring his ego-consciousness to it he must discover a third factor, namely, behind his feeling, a longing for Christ, a longing for ego-reality. Just as our 'I' is present as an ideal above our thinking and as pure will below our desires in the unconscious depth of our soul, so the longing for Christ lives behind our self, the *need* for Christ, as Rudolf Steiner calls it. In order to bring the self that we develop through perception, feeling and knowledge towards Christ, we must free it from its fetters. Free it from its ties to our thinking, feeling and willing, and to a different degree in man and woman. It is more emotional in a woman, more intellectual in a man, and here our 'I' is blocked and may remain in its desperate situation of need right into old age.

We have seen earlier how, in passing judgment, the 'I' comes forward. As long as I make use of perceptions, thoughts and feelings to make my *own* judgment then I am always inserting some part of my ego into the judgment. If however, I learn to hold the ego free so that those elements — be they thoughts, concepts, perceptions, or memories — interact and combine freely so that the world itself judges in me, then my 'I' becomes selfless.

On the one hand I can absorb the world's elements freely and with full consciousness. I make them stir and move within me, I can allow them to relate to each other or to keep apart. If I do not succeed in allowing the elements to work together of their own accord then my 'I' intrudes and has lost its freedom.

On the other hand, my ego is engaged where there is a desire, where my ego is in the background and I surrender to the desire.

I enter the true nature of my 'I' when a pure will arises that never wants anything in particular but follows as soon as something right presents itself. I allow the world to judge through me, and then act in free assent. Thus my consciousness and my will move towards Christ, a strenuous wholesome test. We are free to seek it, free to neglect it.

We discover that the real ego is not found only in the ideals above my thinking, in the pure will below my intentions, not only in the longing for Christ behind my feelings, but that it approaches me as my destiny from the world without. My 'I' is not only in me, it is also in everything that comes towards me as destiny. Here begins quite a different judging, quite a different way of saying yes and no, for insofar as I have learnt to say *yes* to what the world judges in me, insofar as I can say *yes* and put my will at the free disposal of whatever should happen, insofar as I can say *yes* to the movement of the 'I' towards Christ, and insofar as I can say *yes* to my destiny, to that degree my ego will arrive by itself at itself.

One must continually wrestle with oneself and with other people to achieve this genuine yes. The Christ is at work in it. This assent of Christ is the Christian faith. As this assent slowly becomes reality we discover that Christ is not united to the self-consciousness of man — there, man is left free — but to the true nature of the ego. To the question, where is Christ in me? One can answer, he is where the ideals are, the pure will is, the longing for Christ is, where destiny comes towards us. Where the 'I' of man is, there is Christ and where Christ is, there is also the true 'I'.

The threefold, the fourfold star, is in his hand. The assent to Christ which is the deed of the free man's consciousness brings it about that with the entry of the Christ being into consciousness the true 'I' also enters. I am because Christ is in me. Self-consciousness and Christ-consciousness depend on one another and therefore self-consciousness without Christ means the radical endangering of the human 'I' in pride or despair.

The human ego comes forth from God the Father but he has given it to the Son. To the extent that the self is filled with the reality of the 'I' the Christ whom we affirm gives meaning to our destiny. Insofar as I say yes to the Christ, he gives my 'I' a content that comes from him. This is love. Only when the 'I' loves does it become sun. In Christ's hands the 'I' is the star. In reaching out to men, through Christ, the 'I' becomes sun, it becomes warm and luminous; and Christ is resurrected in a human ego.

Just as one can say that the great gift of the mystery of Golgotha is that a human body was resurrected, thereby becoming the seed for the future bodily resurrection of humanity, so also it can be said that through the mystery of Golgotha the 'I' of Christ has done the decisive deed whereby a purer and more independent ego-consciousness may unite with the Christ-consciousness so that we can say with St Paul, 'Not I, but Christ in me'.

The Christ encounter is possible in the way my inner being relates to my physical body, the way my 'I' reaches out from the ideal into discursive thought and rises up out of pure will. The 'Christ in us', spoken in the Communion Service of The Christian Community is a profound occult reality, for the Christ being has entered each human being on earth; on the other hand, it is a growing, a becoming, because Christ creates in man. In this realization the struggle is not only for freedom from the Adversary but also towards the Christ.

The Cross on Golgotha

Good Friday begins in Gethsemane with the agony after midnight, the arrest before dawn, the accusations, condemnations and trial before the high priests. Then comes the death sentence by the Sanhedrin, imprisonment, and the synagogue's attempt to deliver him to the Romans for execution. After the coming and going between Pilate and Herod, Galilee's ruler, and the mockery, Pilate attempts to change the death sentence to flogging, there is political discussion about the kingdom, and Christ Jesus is handed over to the soldiers for ultimate mockery of his kingship with the crown of thorns, the purple cloak and the reed. Ecce Homo! Finally the cry comes, 'Crucify him!'

He who undergoes all this hardly speaks a word. The little he does say is all-embracing. But in decisive moments, he keeps silence. Just before noon, (how was it the cross was so quickly at hand?) the short way is trodden from palace to place of execution. The cross is carried, laid on the ground, the body is stretched upon it, nailed down, the cross is erected and anchored in the earth.

Jesus on the cross: the crucifixion has been represented thousands of times. It was a public spectacle in those days. The friends were there, the enemies, the executioners. Christ on the cross: invisible to man, visible to the spiritual world, the elemental beings of the earth were there, the Adversaries, the heavenly hierarchies, the Father in heaven.

The body hung with arms stretched out and feet together in utmost pain, itself a cross. The blood streaming incessantly, leaving the body, was given to the earth — the earth as a totality of earth, water, air, fire, wind, clouds and light, of mineral, plant, animal and man.

The silent vision becomes a rune, a sign, a word, which had been uttered fourteen hours earlier, 'With the bread, eat my body. With the wine, drink my blood.' What was fulfilled on the cross had begun in that upper room. What is visible for the senses for three hours, the body, is a perfected fruit given to mankind as a seed, a spiritualized form of man. It carries within it the avowal of the divine to this pure body of man, a human body for the human 'I'. Because without 'body' (it does not need to be material, but the form must be human) without its own body an ego cannot be certain of its own being. It would have no foothold. The blood that flows from the cross for three hours and after death through the spear wound, streams into earth and man, a warm wellspring creatively renewing itself. In it flows divine confidence in the substance of man's ego. Because without blood (it need not be material, but the force to create substance for the spiritual being of the ego must have been received) the ego cannot realize itself. It would remain empty.

On the cross, the body speaks the Godhead's confession to man. In the blood the faith of the Godhead speaks to man as eternally flowing trust.

The picture is not complete without a supersensory image. He who places the body and blood of Jesus before mankind is in truth the Christ who allows his divine love to radiate through Jesus, as Christ himself allows the love of the Father to radiate to mankind.

And yet in the silent language of the cross, the human word sounds in its most quiet form. The seven 'I am' sayings of Christ, son of the sun, are woven into the Gospel of St John. Seven words spoken from the cross are shared between the four Gospels. The words of Christ become words of Jesus. They form a mystical symbol, the movement of an ego becoming now a movement of soul vibrating within them. It speaks to the whole world in St John's 'I am' words as a revelation of the sun. The words on the cross relate to man, to our own dying, to the Father, to our body and to our work here on earth.

The first is spoken for those who have to 'celebrate' the execution: 'Father, forgive them; for they know not what they do' (Luke 23:34). The loving word of forgiveness through the Son to mankind.

The second is directed to one who is crucified with Jesus: 'Truly, I say to you, today you will be with me in Paradise' (Luke 23:43). The loving word of comfort from the human being through the Son to the spirit.

The third goes to the people nearest him: 'Woman, behold, your son! . . . Behold, your mother!' (John 19:26f). From man through the Son to man streams the loving word of human fellowship.

Then the word to the Father: 'Father, into thy hands I commit my spirit' (Luke 23:46). The loving word of surrender in the act of death, through the Son to the Father.

Even the need of his own body does not remain unspoken: 'I thirst' (John 19:28). He receives vinegar and gall and he drinks. The sour and bitter draught binds the soul to his body till the last moment, as physical pain did throughout the day. This was the loving word from the Son to the body and the blood. How remote is the first experience in the body after the Baptism in the Jordan and the forty days without food, when the Adversary appeared.

Lastly arises the vision of the total event: that which had been intended from the beginning, lived through, taught, healed and suffered, 'It is finished' (John 19:30). The word of love encompasses the whole deed of life and death: from the ego to the work, from the work to the ego.

If love is that which flows from one being to another, from one world to another, warming and illuminating, these are words of love. The cross on Golgotha is not only a sign of Passion and suffering. With profound meaning the Rosicrucians put seven roses around the cross. The crucifixion is not left out, it has been retained in the black wood of the cross, but the words of love blossom in the seven red roses, which inspired Goethe in his unfinished peom, 'The Mysteries' to ask: 'Who added the roses to the cross?'

And indeed they are seven words. The most mysterious saying of Jesus on the cross is the central one, 'My God, my God, why hast thou forsaken me?' It is absent in Luke and John, we find it in Matthew 27:46, and Mark 15:34 with the note 'at the ninth hour'. What strikes us is the rendering of these words in Hebrew, that is to say, Aramaic, within a Greek Gospel, 'Eli, Eli, lama sabach-thani?' and the interpretation of those present: 'Behold, he is calling Elijah.'

This interpretation belongs to the many misunderstandings of Christ Jesus. He did not call Elijah but expressed the experience of death and of dying. We all die with a different degree of consciousness. What we behold from the outside is experienced by the dying person from the inside. He either slumbers across the threshold half-consciously or he may be blinded by an excess of wakefulness which comes about through the parting of life and body. It also happens that a person remains awake, calm and conscious while he watches from within the parting of the life forces from the body.

We may think of Jesus dying with a selfless and pure consciousness before and after the moment of death on Golgotha, carrying the process within his body, soul and spirit. The word 'Eli' does not refer to Elijah and is rendered 'Eloi' in several manuscripts. The sound 'El', God, is encompassed by the soul in the 'o' and experienced as the God of the ego in the 'i'. It could be translated 'O thou God for my "I",' or 'O thou God of my "I".' Who is the God of Jesus? It is the Christ ego.

The word *lama* does not really just mean 'why' but 'how'. Various manuscripts differ in the Greek transcription. The word 'Eli' is sometimes written as ἠλι elsewhere as ἐλωι (*Elōi*). The second word varies between *lima* (λιμα) and *lama* (λαμα). The third is handed down to us in quite different forms. The scripts have *sabachthani* (σαβαχθανι), *zaphthani* (ζαφθανι) and *zabaphthani* (ζαβαφθανι).

Rudolf Steiner gave two interpretations of this word. One is 'forsaken', the other 'elevated', 'glorified'. Taking them not as opposites but as two sides of the same happening, the saying of Jesus is seen as a true expression of his experience as a human being and of the parting of the Christ-ego from him.

With the entry into Jerusalem, the penetration of Jesus the man was completed and the parting began. The first person to perceive this was the woman in Bethany who washed him with her tears and who anointed him because she felt him to be dying; and he confirmed it in speaking about his burial (John 12:7). The Last Supper would not have been possible if the divine Christ had not already begun to leave the body of Jesus, taking life forces into the bread and wine and passing over into the communion of his disciples. At the arrest in Gethsemane, according to Mark, the figure of a fleeing youth appeared. All through Good Friday the cosmic Christ-being hovered above Jesus, participating in the drama, dwelling finally perhaps only in his heart. On the cross Christ Jesus died out of the man Jesus, who experienced this in full consciousness, with deep amazement saying the words with the one meaning, 'O thou God of my ego, in what glorified manner thou departest from me.'

The other side of the saying is there as well, because Christ completed the deed of redemption in the man Jesus, purified the body from the effects of the Fall, and transformed the soul to the vessel for the Christ-ego — glorifying the whole human being. And so we hear from the cross the other meaning: O thou God of my ego, how thou hast glorified me.

The cross on Golgotha is not only the sign of Passion, of love, but also the sign of a life that grows out of death in the form of a new body and new blood, a glorified man who is resurrected a few days after death. Novalis was close to knowing this secret when he said, 'In death eternal life was known. You are death, you alone give us health.'

Who is death? Who holds the Christ on the cross, who in truth, carries Jesus? The deepest secret of the crucifixion is Death himself. Outwardly death has three faces: rigidity and the end of all that flows, severance of all that holds together, separation from oneself. But Jesus speaks in St John's Gospel of going to the Father. What has death to do with the Father God?

The Old Testament tells of him as the Creator of the world and man, of energy and matter; and the Elohim and Yahweh are his co-creators. The description of the Fall and the image of the expulsion from Paradise can be thought of as if man were thrust out of the protection of God, or as if God withdrew from man. In this way at birth a threshold comes about, forming a bridge between this world and the beyond. Each incarnation weaves the physical and spiritual together. But in death the threshold becomes an abyss, because there is severance, and a realm from which the Father God has withdrawn, that goes through the whole of creation, as a nothing, an emptiness. This is the place in the universe where the Father is not, but death is. In this case, death is a Father who has resigned.

Before Christ came to earth, and entered the realm of death on the cross of Golgotha, the space which the Father had left was occupied unlawfully by the prince of this world and man was caught in his power in death and dying. But at his death, Christ Jesus entered that realm and drove the prince of darkness out. From the moment of his death until the resurrection on Easter morning, the two beings struggled for dominion over death. Victory came to the loving Son, not to the prince of this world. Resurrection belongs fundamentally to the death on the cross.

If a being dies, dying into the Father is experienced as nothingness. Death is destruction when the prince of this world rules; death becomes resurrection when it is filled with the love of his Son. The true cross, seen spiritually, in the power of the abyss; the nothingness between Creator and the created is God himself and the Son fills this abyss with love.

If we see Jesus on the cross, as him who suffers and speaks to us, if we see Christ on the cross, radiating love, then we perceive death as the Father who supports the cross that holds the Son and carries the Man. One cannot think of the cross without the Father. Into the abyss that was kept empty and open by the Father, Christ died; out of the man Jesus, in the parting of body and blood, of body and life, Jesus died.

But through the dying and death of Christ Jesus on the cross, the abyss is no longer empty. It is filled with the substance which the Son carries into death: the love of the Son to the Father, and to mankind. The seven words of love are the expression of a life that conquered death because it transformed it; and love is greater than death.

The Mystery
of the Body of Jesus

It is inadequate to celebrate Easter only on Easter Sunday and perhaps on Easter Monday. On the altars of The Christian Community the mood of Easter is celebrated for forty days, beginning on Easter Sunday. It is expressed in the Easter epistles that open and close the daily communion service, the Act of Consecration of Man, and remains unchanged during these weeks. What, then, is Easter? The presupposition of Easter is Christmas. Christmas is an encounter of the human heart with the loving heart of Jesus Christ. Our consciousness is enkindled by the love of Christ Jesus in each man. As we move away from Christmas into the year, however, a change comes, for we cannot long sustain that profound feeling of love. As the weeks pass man emerges from the inwardness of winter and turns his eyes to the new fertility of the sense world. It must seem that as Christmas recedes the deep feeling for Christ Jesus decreases. There is a reason for this. Our relationship to Christ undergoes a change, not that he distances himself from us, after the nearness of Christmas; on the contrary, he has withdrawn from the sphere of feeling and entered deeper levels of humanity. Even nearer to us than at Christmas, he has receded from our consciousness to enter the substratum where the soul lives. As Passion-tide approaches the condition of man is pronounced from the altar. 'The place of our heart is empty', it is said 'We have lost the spirit that wakens us', and we live in 'the cold spirit-forsaken house of earth'. The words then express a kind of physiology in which sorrow slows our blood and in our breath is 'want' for we lack the true spiritual circumstances in which man should live.

· At Easter, however, this strange physiology of blood and breath is changed and suddenly, 'The grave is empty, the heart is full'. The breath and blood of man unites with the activity of the resurrected one. All at once, he who was resurrected is present. A meditative heart relationship with the course of events has brought about a peculiar fading away, one might say a dying, and now at Easter something breaks open. Throughout the forty days the declaration is made that the Risen One stands close to our soul and spirit, to our blood and heart-beat, our breathing, our body.

Towards the end of a cycle of lectures Steiner said:
Perhaps it has not yet occurred to all those of you who have read the earlier elementary cycles, and so have met with Christian Initiation in its seven stages, that owing to the intensity of the experiences which must be undergone, the effects go right into the physical body. For through the strength and power with which we go through these feelings, it really is at first as if water were washing over our feet, and then as if we were transfixed with wounds. We actually feel as if thorns were pressing into our head; we feel all the pain and suffering of the Crucifixion. We have to feel this before we can experience the Mystical Death, the Burial and the Resurrection,

as these also have been described. Even if we have not gone through these feelings with sufficient intensity, they will certainly have the effect that we become strong and full of love in the right sense of the world. But what we then incorporate can go only as far as the etheric body.

When, however, we begin to feel that our feet are as though washed with water, our body as if covered with wounds, then we have succeeded in driving these feelings so deeply into our nature that they have penetrated as far as the physical body. They do indeed penetrate the physical body, and then the stigmata, the marks of the bleeding wounds of Christ Jesus, may appear. We drive the feelings inwards into the physical body and know that they develop their strength in the physical body itself. We consciously feel ourselves more in the grip of our whole being than if the impressions were merely in the astral body and etheric body.*

In using the word stigmata, Rudolf Steiner places the whole mystery of the human body before us. We can think in this connection of Francis of Assisi, Anna Katharina Emmerich, Therese of Konnersreuth, those people who had such empathy in their soul for Christ Jesus that it worked into their physical body. They demonstrate how different the body is from what present-day science thinks. The nourishment of those so stigmatized, for example, had a totally different character from that of ordinary people. They

* Rudolf Steiner, *From Jesus to Christ*, Rudolf Steiner Press, London 1973

were able to live on the consecrated bread of the Eucharist. This means that the body of a man or woman can be so filled with compassion for Christ Jesus and his earthly fate on Golgotha that blood, tears, glandular activity and metabolism are changed. Scientists have attempted with detailed investigation to discover the causes of stigmata but in vain. Yet the facts exist. Nor ought we to forget that stigmatized people have visions and in connection with festivals experience a loosening of the soul and spirit from the physical body, enabling them to perceive what took place long ago in Palestine. The visions need not correspond exactly with facts, for sensations arising in the soul merge and change the images. Nevertheless, significant insights have been attained. Anna Katharina Emmerich was able to see that the meal which Christ held on Maundy Thursday was not the Passover of the Jews, who celebrated it on Good Friday, but an Essene meal. This has been confirmed by the spiritual investigation of Rudolf Steiner although some things have also been expressed which were not confirmed. The facts show that the human body and blood are quite different from what is commonly believed today.

To understand what took place in the body and blood of Christ Jesus, the resurrection must be seen against the background of the normal human body. Our bodies are extraordinarily complicated. What we carry about with us is not simply material substance, it is inhabited by a 'life' body of forces called in anthroposophy etheric formative forces. Within these lives the soul or astral body, and within this the ego which moulds the soul. These higher members of our being have a reflection in our body. On the one hand the physical body has structural elements, the nervous system, muscles and bones — and on the other hand, physiological processes, sense perception, glandular activity, metabolism. The blood operates between these two triads. The blood is closely related to breathing in a rhythm of one breath to four heartbeats and through the reciprocal action of blood and breathing, man's central organ is the heart. This wonderful organization is enclosed in the skin. The skin is outside, the heart is in the middle, with blood and respiration; then on the one hand we have the physiological process of sense perception, glands, metabolism-digestion, and on the other a system of organs, the nerve, muscle and bone organization. This is a simplified picture of our body.

What is the significance of this physical structure for man? Why do we leave the spiritual world and enter this wonderfully fashioned body? The formative force penetrates the system to construct and maintain it, right into the smallest part of its material appearance. This force appears in the twelvefold division of our whole body: in head, larynx, shoulders, chest, heart, intestines, hips, sexual organs, thighs, knees, lower legs and feet. Underlying this spiritually permeated substance there is an ideal structural form, and it is of great significance that a human being has just such a body and blood. If we did not have a material body, formed in this particular way, our spirit and soul might have very powerful experiences reaching down even into life-activity, without any consciousness of them. Or perhaps we could be conscious, and yet not know of that which has this consciousness — ourselves. For what occurs within us, is only experienced because the spiritual, the soul and the physical forces are reflected in the complicated physical body; and on the other hand, the blood stream is continually circulating, so that we have an enclosed consciousness, perception and feeling of ourselves. We owe our self-consciousness to this body. Why is it so complicated?

Only because in it all the possibilities of spiritual activity are latent. The most manifold sensations of our exclusiveness can be made conscious in the blood stream. The great gift of the pure form of the body penetrates the smallest hair and the minutest cell and is the basis of our separateness, our exclusive self-consciousness. One begins to understand what Novalis meant by the question, 'Who can fathom the profound meaning of the earthly body? Who can say that he understands the blood?' The miracle of man's physical body, blood and human form is so created and integrated that spiritual, soul and bodily life can arise and have meaning in itself.

But this wonderful creation has a totally different side to it. We learn through anthroposophy that the whole evolved structure of body, blood and human form was not divinely intended. Originally man was thought of as a being who would live and remain in a spiritual world, and be no more than a kind of idea in the mind of certain divine beings. The human 'I' was to exist as a kind of sun in the spiritual world, a star through which the thoughts of gods would stream, a companion of the gods. The 'I' should have been an instrument of the world's spirit.

Man's soul should have lived in respiration: as it

breathed in it felt the actions of the gods in itself, expressing them in vowels; and, as it breathed out, it connected itself with the world which is perceived in the working of spiritual beings who would be reflected in consonants. The soul would have been an instrument of the cosmic Logos in which the Logos expressed itself in an inward and human manner.

Nor were the human life forces planned to be as they are today. A continuous realization of life was to arise from the star-like 'I', exhaling the cosmic word. Ethereal form upon ethereal form should have been brought forth, not fixed in enduring shapes. The human being should have had only so much material substance as it generated in its own blood and spiritualized, while the activity of the blood densified and strengthened the experience of the 'I'. Materialization would be momentary so that the 'I' attained a kind of self-awareness, enabling it to feel, along with the divine spiritual beings.

This is what the Old Testament describes as 'Adam in paradise': supersensory man with a radiant ego and an intimate cosmic soul-life filled with the Logos, conjuring forth images in the life forces with the materializing and dematerializing of the blood. This was original man as he appeared to Rudolf Steiner's spiritual perception. The creative, paternal being of God brought forth this human being, the hierarchies united their efforts, and the man of paradise was there.

Then quietly the gods began to withdraw from their work and the beings whom we have called Luciferic intervened in evolution, attacking just at the point where the child-like 'I', weaving within God, was beginning to attain a form of independent life and self-awareness through the blood activity. The Luciferic power succeeded in touching the ego, imbuing it with an impulse to strengthen its individual life. In human terms: Lucifer whispered into the ear of man, 'Be more yourself! Try to feel and to strengthen yourself.' And man did so. The sun-ego was drawn into the breathing, living soul and immediately began to be interested in this soul and the soul in it. The first egotistic self-interest arose and indulgence in the paradisal fruit. A contraction took place between the ego and the life of the soul. The predominance of the ego led to egotism.

As the soul began to experience the activity of the ego in the blood it also began to be interested in the matter that streams into the blood from without and in the matter generated within the blood. A first indication of hunger and thirst appeared which developed into the digestive system. This was a predominance of soul over physiology.

The soul could only achieve this predominance by incorporating life forces into its activity which led to their imbuing themselves more heavily with matter than was originally intended. In consequence, man's glandular activity began to reveal the interaction of matter, life and soul. Consider for example, weeping, laughing or breaking into a sweat. Glandular activity began to develop bodily sensations for the ego and the soul, not only hunger and thirst and enjoyment of matter, but a feeling for the material body, a predominance of physiology over the soul, for example in the power of glands in sexuality.

Life forces were not only experienced within the body but drawn into the outer world and sense perception opened. The Fall occurred when man no longer experienced what happened in his senses, but what was brought from the outer world through them. The material world dominated the spirit.

Originally the different members of the human being were to be more independent, but through the Fall this was lost and a contraction and knitting of the different parts took place. This resulted in a heightened feeling of the self, a heightened experience and relish of matter, and a heightened feeling of man's body and blood as his own property.

The evolution originally intended — that man should slowly and steadily unfold yet remain essentially in the spiritual world — was drawn down into the world of matter. Experience of the self, the body and the world was accelerated. From incarnation to incarnation human souls slipped ever more deeply into matter, particularly after the separation of the sexes, out of which heredity arose. It is true that early man could for centuries perceive the supersensory but he no longer lived within it, he was in material existence as long as his incarnation lasted. He had a kind of memory of pre-earthly existence and a preview of life after death, but the here and now became stronger, his spirituality grew ever darker, the soul more subjective, and the activities of life were directed increasingly towards the earthly. Humanity descended.

First paradise, then the contraction and man's obsession with himself, thirdly the gradual descent at each incarnation, with the lost awareness of what was before birth and after death: these three evolutionary phases placed humanity in a situation which compelled the divine world to ask how the body would affect man as it became even more mineralized.

Matter must really be regarded as a kind of structure, a field formed by beings active below matter, producing atomic forces, magnetism and electricity, and beings who work above it and generate supersensory powers in warmth, colour, tone and scent. When supersensory and subsensory forces and beings act together, influencing and maintaining one another, there arises what we call matter.

There are two different kinds of sense organs. We have those with which we partially perceive the subsensory effects of matter in the sense of touch, the sense of movement, and that of balance. These reveal what comes from the subsensory regions, weight, density, hardness and mass. On the other hand, the higher senses convey what we hear, see and feel as warmth, what we taste and smell, and reveal the qualities which higher beings weave into matter out of the supersensory. To the degree in which physical matter constitutes the bodily nature of man it obtains power over the soul and spirit, and weakens self-experience. We recognize that it loses its unity with the world from which it came. We feel the human being sinking further with each incarnation into what is called 'sickness of sin' in the bodily nature of mankind. The substance of the body draws the soul ever more to the material world, the thought that is attached to this crumbling material becomes ever more intellectual and abstract. It makes feeling subjective and self-indulgent and finally leads man into the illusion that body and 'I' are identical.

Philosophical theories demonstrate this. At first,

man was known to consist of body, soul and spirit, later of body and soul, the soul being allowed spiritual qualities; then just body and soul; then body with soul qualities. Today it is often only body, only matter — with an ideology superimposed. This is a threat. Man has come into the power of the adversary whom anthroposophy calls Ahriman, who entangles him in a material consciousness which puts its faith in matter, and considers only earthly living and dying. If this influence progressed unhindered the true ego-consciousness of man would be extinguished. Man would experience himself as a kind of intelligent animal, taking his being as identical with his body and its life.

Why did the divine beings allow entry first to Lucifer, then to Ahriman? Each individual, as an enclosed entity can become conscious of his spiritual freedom and reach self-determination and responsibility from the depths of personal weakness. This is a fundamental paradox of our earthly existence. The same body that imparts our personality becomes in itself a being that threatens us most deeply.

Before this backcloth stands the figure of Jesus Christ. The man who had body and blood as we do. Was this body subject to the sickness of sin? Did it carry elements that threaten man as a spiritual being? If not, how can the mystery of Jesus's body be understood, the body that did not decay after death but rose again? Let us consider the nature of Jesus, the soul that lived in his body.

We learn through anthroposophy that during the time when man was sinking lower and lower through the seduction of Lucifer and Ahriman, while the originally created spiritual members were changed, and sexual differentiation and reproduction arose, and evolution passed into the stream of heredity, the gods who watched over humanity held back part of the soul of the original Adam, preventing it from descending into matter. They retained it in the spiritual world for thousands of years, while human souls incarnated and with the help of initiates it was guided by spiritual beings until the time was ripe for it to incarnate. It was only when earthly man had sunk deeply into matter that Christ could intervene. The innocent soul who had not participated in the descent was born for the first time as Jesus of Nazareth, the Jesus of the Gospel of St Luke.

A profoundly moving mystery is expressed in the creed of The Christian Community. 'The birth of Jesus upon earth is a working of the Holy Spirit, who, that he might spiritually heal the sickness of sin upon the bodily nature of mankind, prepared the son of Mary to be the vehicle of the Christ.' The Holy Spirit, shining out as the most exalted member of the Trinity, guides the pure human soul of Jesus, untainted by the Fall, out of the spiritual world. This divine being sees to it that the child enters the right family, that its conception is not burdened with passion and lust, that the parents are brought together in dream and sleep. When the infant soul, the Jesus child of Luke's Gospel is born on earth, his mother perceives that the child carries the original language of paradise in his soul. When the soul felt itself as a vessel of the Logos, permeated by the sevenfold divine, it could utter truth in seven vowels and express the structure of the world in twelve consonants. The Jesus child speaks the original language of the soul and his mother understands it.

To heal spiritually 'the sickness of sin upon the bodily nature of mankind', could only be possible if this child did not suffer the contraction that arose through the Fall, if his spirit was the sun and the stars and was ready to let the divine shine through itself; if the life forces had power to generate life and the body was not overcome by the darkness of matter. We must have the courage to regard the body of Jesus from the first breath as something unique, where the division of the Fall was not present in principle.

This soul had from childhood the possibility of steeping itself to the depth of infinity in everything around it. There are deep souls and superficial human souls; but listening to this one soul reveals his ability to sympathize with all men around him. If anyone experienced the darkening of man's spirit, the weakening of the soul, the infinite suffering of his fellow man that person was Jesus. In his lectures *The Fifth Gospel*, Rudolf Steiner speaks of the 'genius of the heart.' Jesus himself had no part in sickness and Rudolf Steiner describes the suffering that he went through because of the way humanity lived in his time. Through its intensity the consciousness, the soul and life forces of the man Jesus were illumined, the body was almost transparent. From his childhood until his Baptism in the Jordan at the age of thirty, Jesus felt the sickness of sin in his fellow human beings with deep sympathy and also with readiness to sacrifice his will to whatever would come to him. The vehicle for redemption was prepared by his thirtieth year.

The preparation for the resurrection is threefold: in

body, soul and spirit. To the Jesus-soul described in St. Luke's Gospel, a second soul is guided by destiny. Rudolf Steiner speaks in detail of this second Jesus, whose childhood is narrated by St Matthew.* When the two boys had shared their childhood in Nazareth, there followed a union of the ego, the 'I' of the older one with the soul of the younger, in their twelfth year. The youth of Jesus went through three phases, three spheres of life, the Jewish, the heathen and the Essene. In all, Jesus experienced with pain the consequences of the Fall, accumulating up to his time.

Over the centuries, Judaism had created eugenic conditions whereby the continuity of priests, kings and prophets upheld the divine voice in human hearts. Jesus found that through the Fall the change in the physical structure had silenced it. The suffering brought upon him by spiritual blindness and the arid legality in the hardened hearts and minds of Abraham's seed plunged his soul into deep sorrow for his people.

In later wanderings among the bordering heathen tribes, he found that the cult of the life-giving nature gods had died out and that life forces in man and nature had succumbed to demonic illnesses. A feeling of deep powerlessness gripped his soul in the realization that he was not able to help them.

In the third period of his life, before he was thirty, Jesus entered into an intimate relationship with the Essene order which he had known earlier. He felt that the pure soul-life of the Essenes could remain free of

---

* *The Fifth Gospel.* See also Emil Bock, *Kindheit und Jugend Jesu*, Verlag Urachhaus, Stuttgart 1980.

demons. But he saw that through their practice the demons were all the more strongly drawn to other men. The strict Essene way of life produced sickness elsewhere. Again, Jesus had to experience his powerlessness in the face of sickness, demonry and spiritual blindness.

The effect of the Fall on the body of the Jews, on the life forces of the heathens and the striving of the souls of the Essenes was felt as guilt and suffering by Jesus more profoundly than ever before. He recognized that divine redemption must be offered to every part of man's being at one and the same time.

Longing and suffering then led him to John the Baptist by the Jordan where through his pain the ego of Jesus was pressed out of his body, passed into the spiritual world and the Christ-being entered into his body and blood. The power of the earthly ego over the soul, egotism, was extinguished and divine selflessness filled the soul of Jesus. Out of the helplessness of the ego in face of the Fall in body, life and soul appeared divine authority as response to the longing for redemption. Now the God was present and Jesus received power to free us from sin.

The Christ ego immediately began to work in the soul of the man Jesus. The soul, that carried something of paradise within became more independent of the body, finally attained complete union with the stars and the twelvefold Logos. The Gospels speak not only of the divine world but of the nourishment that issued through it from the soul of Jesus as food for souls and for whole groups of people in the feeding of the five thousand. The twelve baskets which were filled with bread are an image of the healing and perfecting of the soul of Jesus. The disciples saw Christ walking on the Sea of Galilee. This image shows the soul freed from the predominance of the life-forces — it can walk freely over the waves of the ethereal watery life forces without sinking into them. The narratives of the feeding of the five thousand and the vision of his walking on the sea describe the soul that had regained the state divinely intended for mankind, and added to the paradisal being an infinite compassion. Through the Christ ego the soul of Jesus became bread, became autonomous, free of the predominance of the lower self, free from the predominance of body and life.

When the Christ ego worked further down into the life forces of Jesus, life-giving, healing forces streamed out, so that finally the life body became free and paradisal again. No longer in need of the light of the spirit and soul, it began to shine forth itself: he 'led them up a high mountain apart. And he was transfigured before them, and his face shone like the sun, and his garments became white as light.' (Matt. 17:1f) A free, selfless and compassionate soul allowed life-bearing forces to ray through it.

The ego of Christ worked deeper still into the substance of the body, healing the restless craving nature of material substance and converting it into a mineral selfless state. As Christ Jesus rode into Jerusalem on the ass, the people perceived the radiance of his skin, his body had become transparent. The 'Hosanna' of the people is joy over what they half-consciously saw shining from him.

To the degree that paradisal man was restored — the ego becoming sun-like and the soul star-like, the life forces sun-like and the body like pure crystal — the members of his being no longer had to adhere together as in an ordinary human being where the parts are knitted together. What had to happen? Death came. This paradisal man could not remain on earth, the material substance threatened to slip away from him, and from one or the other side he had to accept help. It was given to him. In Gethsemane an angel helped him to hold body and soul together; the traitor Judas embraced him, gave him a passionate kiss of love and imparted the strength to live for the remaining few hours, that he might die on the cross.

Finally, the wounds were of great significance for the resurrection. Jesus was tied with a rope when he was taken prisoner, beaten before the high priests, scourged, crowned with thorns and made to bear the cross. The meaning of pain is most evident when the nails were hammered in, compressing this soul once more into the body, and finally when he is given vinegar and gall. The innocent body that only outwardly presented a material veil, and that appeared as a human body in its pure form, was given power and substance through its wounds until death overcame it, the members separating as the blood of the sacrifice flowed into the earth. This was indeed a real death.

We must surmise that during the three days after death the ego had full Father-consciousness and penetrated the earth, shining as the sun. Anna Katharina Emmerich wrote how he penetrated the earth in the evening of Good Friday, the night of the sabbath. 'He goes through the rock.' The independent soul gathered the forces of the stars out of the cosmos into the depths of the earth. The life forces did not ebb away into the ethereal world as they do with every normal human being. This ethereal body that carried all the events of the three and a half years as a memory tableau, coalesced with its own realm of life, filled with images, forces and being. Each encounter, each word, each deed of Christ during the three years on earth formed its own sphere of life forces within the earth. Something that only Jesus himself could have, however, was added to the blood from the wounds: faith flowed in the blood, trust in the universal process of evolution transformed it to spirit — an aura of radiant trust now clothed the earth.

Disciples took down the body, wrapped it in a shroud; it was anointed with spices and placed in the tomb. It was already pure light. Everything in the material substance of this body that could be spiritualized and ensouled was transformed into spirit during the three days of silence in the grave. Everything that belonged to the subsensory world, the heaviness and the dust, fell from the body like ash when the earthquake shook. The earth began to open and close, to breathe and to sigh, taking the ash through a fissure into the body of the whole earth. Since that time it has been working as a ferment in the gradual spiritualization of earthly substance.

The substance rises up on Easter morning. It rejoins the life forces and the soul as spiritual substance. This is the mystery of the resurrection. The transformation of the innocent body of Jesus, the return to paradise, has meaning only if the true Form of man remains upright.* The true human Form ensures that

* Rudolf Steiner calls this pure Form the 'phantom' in his lecture cycle, *From Jesus to Christ*.

a human being is self-contained and will rise from the grave. It receives physical substance and transforms it, uniting again with the life forces, that the Christ 'I' may shine in the bodily resurrection like a sun in its own realm. The innocent body of Jesus of Nazareth, permeated by the Christ, is the presupposition and the reality of resurrection on Easter morning.

This body remained by the earth for forty days, until Christ again made a sacrifice, giving the forces of resurrection into the ethereal and astral layers of the earth as seed for renewal. The trust in the world that flowed in the blood and our standing in the reality of the reanimated pure Form are the moral and spiritual background of what we call the body and the blood of Christ. At the centre is Christ Jesus himself. Sacrificing himself for mankind and the world, he can densify his body and blood at any time and place on earth and pass it into sacramental bread and wine, for the bodies and blood of men. As Christ strengthens our love to him it goes over into our breathing, our pulse, our blood; and thus our body shares in the healing of the sickness of sin. Man's nature is freed from the weight of matter and gains the power to spiritualize part of our body. This takes place when we receive the sacrament of Communion and when we intensify Christ's love in our hearts, uniting our soul with his, so that it works in our breathing and in our blood leading to our experience of the healing of the spiritual-physical body.

Christ's Resurrection

These two words have a most powerful content and form the basis of Christianity. Christmas is the first foundation: the Word became flesh, behind it stands the sacrifice of a divine being who leaves heaven and takes on life on earth. The second foundation is Easter: the death and resurrection of Christ. The third comes with Ascension and Whitsun and has an effect for the earth and mankind as a whole.

Looking at the pattern of Christianity, one can get the impression that from the orbit of the cosmos something contracts into a centre where the great mystery takes place: death, burial, resurrection. This centre will work out into the infinite widths of space in future. It is like one gigantic divine breath of life.

For the last two thousand years Christianity has taken these events for granted. For Christian hearts and souls the fact itself was not as important as the salvation and the pious, personal relationship of a Christian to his Saviour. People asked, 'What does it mean for myself, for my soul and for my existence?' To contemplate this being itself, apart from what it means for me, was neglected. Let us look at the resurrection selflessly and objectively, to see what happened.

We depend on pictures drawn in the Gospels in contemplating the resurrection. A peculiar characteristic meets us, when we accompany the central figure in our thought. Christ Jesus during Passion Week, is seen day by day, being led through the crowd on Good Friday. We do not even need artists and their countless representations of the crucifixion. Everybody can follow the Gospel events with an inner eye and hear him speak. Behind the pictures, currents of strength show a true esoteric event. Walking imaginatively with Joseph of Arimathea, Nicodemus and the women as they take the body from the cross, we visualize the shroud, the spices and ointment, the corpse in repose, perhaps hands folded, inside the tomb.

Yet on Easter morning we hear, 'The grave is empty!' Or we can see, as John describes, the napkin that was about the head, not lying with the linen clothes, but folded in a place by itself. But the central figure is gone. Strange how the Gospels mirror the event of the resurrection in the circumference, veiling from our eyes what really happened. Matthew, Mark and Luke show the women on the way to the tomb. Careful reading is needed to see who these two or three women really are, for they are not the same in each case. In the thought and soul of every group the event is mirrored and yet remains veiled for us. In Matthew we find the guards become 'like dead men' on Easter morning. In John we see two disciples, Peter and 'the other', the circle of people is there and what happens inside them reflects the fact that the grave is empty.

These people are not the only witnesses, the Gospels go beyond them in describing how the cosmos shares in the events. On Good Friday the darkening of the sun affects all earthly life, green plants turn grey, flowers lose their colour, the sun is hidden, the earth is dark and from the third hour onward — the moment of death — an earthquake takes place. Mankind, cosmos and earth participate. Even the hierarchies appear at the grave. According to Matthew, in a vision given to the women an 'angel of the Lord' rolls away the stone and sits upon it. Mark records that a 'young man', dressed in a white robe is sitting on the right side. In the empty tomb of Luke's Gospel the women behold two men in 'dazzling apparel' who speak to them. John tells of Mary Magdalene gazing into the dark chamber and seeing two angels where the body has lain, one at the head and one at the feet. Step by step, the divine world shares in the events. But still the resurrection cannot be seen. Except in John's Gospel we hear only, 'He is not here!' This is the *hagios topos*, the holy place, where he was laid, but is no longer — he is risen. It may be a Greek, a Latin, an Aramaic or a Hebrew 'He is risen', but the consciousness of the Angels, Archangels, Archai and the Spirit of Form who rolled away the stone, is filled with the deed of resurrection. The angels know of it and pass it over into the souls of the women who do not know how to comprehend it.

In every picture of Easter morning the challenging image of the empty grave stands at the centre. Where is he? In the mind of Mary Magdalene this delicate question works its way to consciousness and suddenly he is there. The empty space is filled with real content from an unexpected direction. It is a purely spiritual touch, 'Mariam', and then 'Rabbouni'. The 'I' of the woman is addressed and she tries to understand. The atmosphere is such that she supposes him to be the gardener — why the gardener? Someone who cares for life? At last she realizes that it is the Risen One.

But he says, 'I have not yet ascended to the Father' (John 20:14-18). Resurrected but not yet ascended — a strange distinction. The Risen One is still like a seed, in the picture of the gardener who cares for life.

The day passes. Luke (24:13-35) tells of two men, Cleopas and his friend who walk in the evening from Jerusalem to Emmaus which lies a few miles to the north-west across the hills of Mizpah open toward the Mediterranean. At sunset Christ 'appeared in another form' (Mark 16:12). We must think of a continually changing presence. He is no longer the gardener, but one who walks *with* the two disciples. Pictures of the Old Testament arise as they walk and the prophecy of the Son of Man, who has to suffer, die and rise again begins to make sense. He was like a companion who can give meaning to the strange and unknown; he gives meaning and so transforms. The wonderful scene in the inn room follows, where they say, 'Stay with us, for it is toward evening and the day is now far spent.' They break bread and in that moment their eyes are opened and they recognize him fully.

Mary Magdalene recognized him when he spoke her name, the disciples in the moment of transubstantiation. The aura of the bread shone when he was present, but in the next moment he was gone. It is as if the resurrection still continues. Cleopas and his friend return to Jerusalem and to the disciples in the house of Mark gathered behind closed doors. In the late evening of Easter Sunday the vision becomes an absolute presence (Luke 24:36-43; John 20:19-23). 'Peace be with you!' He breathes on them and says:

Receive the Holy Spirit, through me you will be able to share it. Something has been formed, but the process of resurrection has not ended.

Eight days later the disciples experience the opposite of Mary Magdalene when she is told not to touch (John 20:24-29). Christ speaks to Thomas, 'Put your finger here, and see my hands; and put out your hand, and place it in my side'. If we do not take this difference seriously we shall misunderstand the Gospels. They describe the self-realization of the Risen One in a spiritual body which has an intensity that reaches to the human sense of touch. Here is a power going beyond the present moment, so that Thomas immediately says, 'My Lord and my God!' Authority has been given 'over all flesh'.

In the scene that follows at the Lake of Galilee in the early dawn (John 21:1-23), when the disciples recognize his presence at the coal fire, the destiny of Peter is challenged after the meal. ' "Do you love me? ... when you were young, you girded yourself and walked where you would; but when you are old, you will stretch out your hands, and another will gird you and carry you where you do not wish to go." (This he said to show by what death he was to glorify God.)' The words to Peter, 'If it is my will that he remain until I come, what is that to you?' show not only the power over flesh, but the power over human destiny, far into the future.

At length the remarkable time when the disciples live together with the Risen One comes to an end. Forty days are soon past. The Gospels leave no doubt that the way the Risen One lived with the disciples, the women and the people who surrounded him, was absolutely unique, beginning on Easter morning and ending on Ascension Day.

The resurrection is a process and the Gospels tell us nothing about it: at first they leave the picture empty, they show what happened around it but the centre remains hidden and how the resurrection took place is an enigma. Then they show the Risen One in his continually changing appearance.

Without its background the secret of the resurrection cannot be understood at all. Man's earthly condition is the condition of the resurrection. Only with the greatest spiritual effort can the power of matter to a certain degree be loosened — if this is desired but many people do not desire it. Man cannot master the substance of his body. But the resurrection is a bodily process. Incarnation in a human body is a continuous process, beginning at birth, deepening throughout life, loosening in death. We can understand why, after death, the connections with matter continue and mankind can be drawn into the realm of bodily decay, where after death he has no strength to keep his soul together. On the other hand, when, in death, the body no longer acts as a mirror then man is not able to remain awake and conscious within the spiritual world.

If we consider the whole picture of our embodiment, resulting from our cosmic condition and its threat to our spiritual existence, we can understand that this threat brings sorrow to mankind and challenges the gods. An immense sacrifice has been offered by Christ, incarnating as a human being like us with all the possibilities of weakness, temptation and change that are ours since the Fall. The mystery of

Golgotha was a deed that entered the core of human existence and cancelled the Fall. The resurrection therefore is not only what happened on Easter morning. It began at the Baptism in the Jordan when Christ entered the man Jesus. The Christ is not obliged to let his consciousness be the reflection of a human body. Consider how *we* become conscious, how as children we fall asleep, and awake to the body and the external world. The Christ enters in full consciousness and does not need physical support from the body. He bears wakefulness majestically in himself.

The first effect of this is that he feels immediately how vulnerable man's nature is. The Gospels call it an encounter with the Adversaries. Another effect is that this wide-awake, sun-filled 'I' immediately begins to eradicate the effects of the Fall on this body. The evangelists leave us in no doubt as to how it is done. The soul of the man Jesus is changed through the presence of the Christ, becoming bread for humanity, in the bountiful selflessness described as the feeding of the five thousand. As the divine spirit pervades the life forces they are no longer in danger of entering too deeply into matter, nor will they dissipate at death into cosmic space. His life forces become like the sun and radiate on Mount Tabor as the disciples see at the Transfiguration. The divine being enters even into man's skin and bones, until the pure formative forces are free and the genuine Form can begin to live. Matter is taken into the divine being, into this body in which a god dwells, and is completely transformed.

Matter has its own secrets. Nowadays one sees

matter either as a crystal or as particles, as electromagnetism. Material substance reveals its inner side, however, only when it is present in a human body and not as it appears in plants, animals and minerals. It reveals its true nature in man, its ability on the one hand to evolve crystalline forces, to reflect so that consciousness can arise, and on the other hand to transform inasmuch as it can be taken into the body and be discarded again. But where a spiritual authority enters and a divine being penetrates material substance it can dissolve matter. Today, we have difficulties in thinking of the resurrection of Christ because we believe so firmly in matter that it never occurs to us that the laws of nature — which are the expression of *hardening* processes — can also be reversed.

The Christ intervenes in the *soul* of Jesus and creates the opposite of egotism, selfishness and indulgence in materialism; namely, nourishing powers of love. Christ intervenes in the *life forces* of Jesus so that they become the opposite of that which binds them to matter. They become creative and sun-like. Finally, the divine being invades *matter* within the form of a human body and this form is made whole, matter itself is spiritualized into the new body. What falls away from this human body is only dust and ash.

Perhaps we can now reconstruct the whole event of the resurrection. As Christ separated from Jesus in death, a body was laid in the tomb that was quite different from the bodies of other people. Here the pure spiritual Form of man's physical body was reconstituted whole, and after being anointed with spices and shrouded according to Jewish ritual its material substance disintegrated very quickly. On the one hand it was transparent like crystal, on the other brittle like fine dust. Rudolf Steiner describes how after the corpse had lain in the tomb for three days, it had undergone an essential change. When the tomb was shaken by the earthquake, currents of air blew through the grave and the earth inhaled the dust that had fallen from the body, and the pure Form rose from the grave filled with that part of matter which reflects, which was able to be transformed, and was free from dust and ashes. The old words of the Protestant Church, 'Earth to earth, ashes to ashes, dust to dust' declare a certain hope that the spirit form rises from the grave.

The resurrected body that leaves the tomb empty and cannot be seen in the beginning has entirely new qualities, powers and abilities. Firstly, we have a body with a centre of gravity, we must brace ourselves all the time against this centre of gravity and maintain our balance on the ground we walk upon. Imagine a body whose centre is not subject to the earth's gravity, and also not to a centrifugal flight into space, but sustains its own force, rises and falls of itself, hovers. Where he was wounded the body of Christ Jesus bears five spiritual centres of force. The soul entered these most deeply in pain. There are also the wounds from the crown of thorns and the scourging. These processes lead to spiritual densification through pain and the wounds become the spiritual centres on which he moves. He is neither drawn to the centre of the earth nor to the periphery of space. He holds himself within himself and the five centres of force light up as sources of spiritual power.

Secondly, we human beings with our heavy bodies are obliged to eat. Of the Resurrected One the opposite is true: a body that nourishes itself, from which streams of life flow, can give each piece of bread blessed on the altar an aura of spiritual nourishing life.

Thirdly to this is added an authority so great that he could densify his spiritual forces into a kind of perceptibility. Thus did the Risen One appear to the people who could see him.

The new Man has arrived! We should not only think of what this means to us, but also try to make the event more comprehensible and real in itself. This can only be done if we are aware that our soul is continually in danger of losing itself in matter or withdrawing from the world and losing earthly consciousness. Let us look at Christ Jesus whose consciousness rests sun-like in itself and is not just the reflection of a body. It radiates! His soul no longer depends on an increased experience of self. Consider a melancholic or hysteric person in whom we see the need for self-assertion, the experience of the self, in extreme form. The soul of Jesus is the opposite where the Christ gives out enduring love and radiates substance.

The fact is that the Risen One existed, the divine Christ was able to take Jesus into himself. Just as one can say that Jesus, the man, embodies the Christ during the three years and that the Christ prepared the resurrection within him for three years, changing him step by step, so likewise one can say that on Easter morning the Christ took Jesus fully into himself so that now one being is present: the Risen One. But that may be too rigid, for he said, 'I am the resurrection and the life'. The image and concept of the Risen One together with the resurrection, show this unique event to be the source from which resurrection can rise again and again eternally. One can really say: Christ is the resurrection.

This became fact when after forty days he transformed the Risen One into the resurrection. This implies power over his own consciousness, over his own creating loving soul, over his self-renewing resurrection body. This power and impulse of the resurrection poured out over the earth. Since then the resurrection has lived in the sphere around the earth. The risen Christ can consolidate himself at any moment and appear or work for one person in one way and for another in a different way. In St John's last appearance of the Risen One, impulses of destiny appear and as the Christ shows one disciple his way and another disciple quite a different way, so does he prepare for each individual his very own resurrection. A world-creating impulse goes out, that works in each individual human being uniquely.

Ascension
by Friedrich Benesch

Benesch examines in detail the nature of the physical event as embodiment of spiritual significance. He presents us with a stimulating account of clouds and the conclusions reached are startling, yet satisfying to both religious and scientifically inclined.

Whitsun
by Friedrich Benesch

This book shows how, in concrete terms, Whitsun is both a celebration of the free individual and of the brotherhood of man.

Festivals in North and South
by Evelyn Francis Capel

Should the Christian festivals be celebrated at the same time all over the world or should they follow the course of the seasons which are opposite in the two hemispheres?

Floris Books